Digital Marketing Glossary

- **A Hit**: A single webpage consists of multiple files like plain text, images, videos, etc. A website page hit is the retrieval of those files from a web server.

- **Event**: An event can be simply defined as an activity that occurs on a website. Example clicks, page view, form submissions, etc.

- **Website Visit**: A truly unique series of page requests by an IP address which is placed on the browser cookie. A visit is considered one visit as long as the events (page views, clicks, etc.) are 30 minutes or less closely together.

- **Unique Visitor**: A visitor who has approached a particular website for the first time. This parameter is important as it gives website owner, an insight on what's the percentage of new visitors versus the returning website visitors.

- **Impression**: From an online media perspective, an 'Impression' is the number of times an 'Ad' is fetched, whether or not that Ad is clicked.

- **Data**: Data is nothing but the facts collected for a reference or for an analysis.

- **Page Views**: A page view is defined as an event when a user visits a particular page on your website whenever it is fully loaded.

- **Returning Visitor**: A website visitors who have made at least one prior visit to a particular website, generally identified by cookies or authentication.

- **Bounce Rate**: A single page visit by a website visitor who does not interact further with that website. The website visitor generally navigates away from the website after viewing only one page. A higher bounce rate is not healthy as far as website ranking on the search engine is concerned.

- **Average Page View Duration**: An average amount of time, a website visitor spends on a website.

- **Organic Search Result**: Internet search results after a user put a search query over the search engine, resulting in the display of relevant search results. The organic search results are free of charge unlike paid advertisements, called Adwords. Also called S.E.O.

- **Keyword**: A word or a phrase which describes the content in a web page is referred to as a 'Keyword'. Search engine matches the user's query on a search engine with a keyword to fetch the result which is both relevant and a high-quality piece of information.

- **Pay Per Click**: Pay per click, also known as P.P.C, is a paid advertising platform where a website pays a sum of money to list on a search engine result pages(S.E.R.P).

- **Session Duration**: It is the average amount of time, a website visitor spend for each visit. It is calculated as the sum of the duration of all the sessions divided by the total number of sessions.

- **Click Through Rate**: Click Through rate is defined as the ratio of the number of times a user clicks on your ad to the number of times that ad is shown. Example if an ad is shown 1000 times, and if it receives 10 clicks, then the Click Through Rate(C.T.R) will be 10/1000*100% which is equal to 1%.

  Click Through Rate is a very important parameter to gauge how your website keywords and ad copies are performing. A high CTR is an indication of how relevant do the internet users find your ads.

- **Landing Page**: A landing page is generally the static page on a website which is intended with an objective of converting your website users into subscribers. In other words, a landing page is where your website visitors end-up after they click on your Ad.

- **Session**: A session is a data related to a visitor who is browsing a website, including multiple page views as well. A session ends on the midnight of the same day that session was initiated or after 30 minutes of inactivity.

- **Tracking Code**: The analytics tracking code is a JavaScript code which collects the data from the website and sends it to the analytics tool for real-time monitoring.

- **Exit Rate**: Exit Rate and Bounce rate seem to be similar but they are actually not!! Exit Rate generally applies to specific pages on a website, i.e the exit pages. In other words, the page that the user viewed just before leaving your website. High exit rates are not good, however, these metrics provide an insight on which areas of your website needs improvement.

- **AdWords**: Adwords is Google's advertising platform where businesses bid on specific keywords to make their ads appear on the first page of the search engine result.

- **Blogging**: An art of writing a piece of valuable information which could benefit the users. A blog is an informative content in the form of text, pictures, and videos.

- **Content Marketing**: Content marketing is an act of creating, publishing, and distributing the valuable information to the audience in the form of content.

- **Call-to-Action**: Call-to-action is used extensively in marketing campaigns to provoke an immediate response from the website visitor with the help of a button.

- **Influencer Marketing**: Influencer marketing focus on influential people who have a strong influence on the potential customers.

- **Crawler**: A crawler is a computer program that visits a website and reads the data on it along with other information and conveys the result to the search engine to index that website. Some of the major search engines across the globe also call it a 'Spider' or a 'Bot'.

- **CPM(Cost Per Mille)**: C.P.M is most commonly referred to as 'Cost Per Thousand Impressions'. This advertising platform is more suitable for a well established brand name like 'ICICI Lombard', 'Maxis Telecom', Microsoft', 'Oracle', 'Volvo' and so on.

  It is calculated as:

  The amount of money spent on Ads/Total number of Ad Impressions * 1000

Job Opportunities in Digital Marketing

There is a prediction of having more than 1.5 lac job opportunities in digital marketing by 2020, according to the "Times of India". All of those who are already practicing digital marketing or those who are working as a digital marketer, are bound to be in a strong position to make a huge growth in near future.

Apart from looking for various job opportunities in digital marketing, you can also start freelancing on various job portals like upwork.com, guru.com, freelancer.com, remote.com, and so on, after you gain some experience in digital marketing.

Let's take a look at various job opportunities in digital marketing;

- **SEO Executive/Manager**: The role of an SEO professional involves implementing SEO Strategy (both On-Page and Off-page), while continuously monitoring search ranking on the first page of the Google search engine.

  The person is also responsible for researching and analyzing competitor's links and their strategies to rank on the first page on a search engine. SEO executive is also expected to handle the search engine friendly content part on their own.

  SEO executives/managers are in high demand and therefore organizations are willing to pay high remunerations to those who have a rich experience in handling SEO strategy. An SEO executive who carries 1 year of working experience is offered an average salary of 3 lacks per annum.

- **SEM Executive/Manager**: A "Search Engine Marketing" specialist is expected to have a strong understanding of the concepts, strategies, policies and the best practices while creating a content that would result in winning a bid over the competitors for a particular "keyword".

  SEM professional is also expected to have a strong knowledge in Google Analytics. The average salary that is offered to an SEM Manager is 4-5 lacks/annum for a person who has 1-2 years of experience.

- **E-mail Marketing Executive/Manager**: An e-mail marketer is expected to manage the implementation and measurement of various email marketing campaigns. The person is also responsible for carrying effective A/B testing strategies for higher R.O.I (Return on Investment), while carrying a sound knowledge and working experience on various email marketing tools like Aweber, Mail Chimp, Zoho CRM, Drip, and so on.

The person holding at least 2 years of experience as an email marketer can be offered an average salary of 4 lakhs/annum.

- **Affiliate Marketer**: An "Affiliate Marketing" is a digital marketing concept which lets an individual or an organization to earn a commission by promoting other business's products or services. Affiliate marketer is expected to possess a sound knowledge on advertising industry, technologies and pricing models.

  An Affiliate marketing manager on the other hand leads a team of affiliate marketers and is also responsible to achieve the desired ROI. An individual who possess more than 1 year of experience as an affiliate marketer can expect an average salary of 3 lakhs/annum.

- **Social Media Executive/Manager**: A social media marketing (SMM) manager is responsible for handling social media blogs and posts, writing various articles for forums and classifieds websites.

  Apart from these basic job responsibilities, an SMM manager is also accountable for monitoring social media activities on various platforms like LinkedIn, Facebook, Twitter, Instagram, etc. A skilled professional having more than one year of experience is entitled for an average salary of 3.5 lakhs/annum.

- **Web Developer/Designer**: Almost all the digital marketing agencies require web designers of web developers as a part of their team to help serve the digital marketing services to their clientele. Depending on your skill set and relevant experience in various tools like Java, PHH, My SQL, CSS, Bootstrap, etc. widely used in website design and development, you can find a good opportunity with some of the most reputed digital marketing agencies.

  On an average, a PHP developer with 2 years of experience can be offered a salary of 4 lacks per annum

- **Content Marketing Manager**: Content marketing is another form of digital marketing where the useful and relevant content is created, published and being distributed online to attract the audience and ultimately generate action from that audience.

  A content marketing manager is responsible to devise marketing strategies aimed for driving traffic that deliver sales for an organization. The person is also accountable to create useful content, and systematically distribute that content to various discussion forums, social channels, etc. Similar to the salary offered to a PHP developer, a Content Marketing Manager can be offered an average remuneration of 4 lacks/annum.

- **<u>Digital Marketing Manager</u>**: A digital marketing manager is responsible for the organization's entire digital marketing efforts. The person develops, implements and manages marketing campaigns to promote products and/or services.

  The role, however differs from organization to organization; also depends on the type of industry the organization targets to market their products or services. Since you are reading this post, I am sure you would also like to work as a "Digital Marketing Manager" someday.

  You must have at least 3-4 years of experience in handling various digital marketing campaigns to apply for this position with an organization.

There are an ample number of other opportunities as well, apart from the above mentioned. Some people do not look to work with an organization. They rather want to provide their own services (freelancing) after gaining some experience on digital marketing campaigns and strategies.

Digital marketing is a booming career with ample advancement opportunities because there are inadequate number of digital marketing professionals whereas the demand is very high. If you plan to be a digital marketing professional in near future, you are on a right track.

Ways to become a digital marketer

Digital Marketing is perhaps more in demand as compared to other available job roles across the globe, and is bound to create more than 1,50,000 jobs by the year 2020. There is however, a substantial gap between the availability of Digital Marketing jobs in the market and the available talent to fill those jobs. Also, the demand for digital marketing experts will keep on increasing exponentially.

If you are looking to become a digital marketing expert someday, you need to start understanding various opportunities in digital marketing, followed by grasping the concepts in digital marketing and implementing those practically.

Since there is no such government recognized degree in "Digital Marketing" so far; you should either go for a course or you can choose to learn and implement digital marketing concepts by your own. It has become easier to learn and implement digital marketing now, more than ever.

The primary reason being the availability of free online resources in the form of blogs, video platforms like "YouTube", and some free online courses which can get you started on your blogging journey.

Let me share some of the most effective methods to help you to choose a right path to become a digital marketer.

- ***Enrol yourself in a digital marketing program***: There are various Digital Marketing courses available in the market where you can get theoretical and practical knowledge about digital marketing.

  Some of those courses are Online while some are Class-Room based. As per your convenience, you can choose either of them.

  You can go for an online course if you are not willing to travel all the way to the training centre. Some people, however, do not feel comfortable attending an online lecture and thus are more comfortable visiting the centre.

  I personally like Class-Room based training because the trainer is going to be right in front of us and we can ask any number of questions and implement those, real-time.

  There are various digital marketing courses available in the market, these days. I would like to mention some of the best institutes you can approach;

Digital Technology Institute(DTI), New Delhi

'DTI' is led by Mr. Anup Prasad, an M.B.A graduate, possessing more than 10 years of experience in digital marketing. The main feature of their digital marketing program is the 'HTML' training, which is included in their digital marketing program. I have personally attended a couple of Demo Classes with the institute and found it worth going for.

The institute has an average student rating of *4.9/5* out of 288 reviews on Google.

Located in Janakpuri (west), they offer the course for 25000 only. The main Highlights of the Digital Marketing Course from this institute are:

- 3 Free Demo classes.

- Hands-on Practical experience.

- Internship opportunities.

- Placement Assistance.

- Workshop and Seminar Invites.

- Free Digital Marketing tools, worth 68000 INR.

Edu Pristine

Edu Pristine provides online and classroom trainings for international certifications in Finance, Accounting, Analytics, Digital Marketing, Project Management and Six Sigma. It offers "Digital Marketing Master Program" comprising of more than 100 hours of lectures and practical sessions. The program also includes Soft Skills Training and 100% placement assistance.

The cost of "Digital Marketing Master Program" is 60000 INR (inclusive of G.S.T), whether you go for classroom training or live virtual training. The key features of the program are:

- 80 hours instructor led training.

- Simulations for real-life practice.

- 1 Live Website Deployment.

- 1 domain name.

- 1 business e-mail account.

The institute has an average student rating of *3.6/5* out of 103 reviews on Google.

Digital Vidya is a known brand in online digital marketing training, claims to have trained more than 30,000 participants. Apart from digital marketing, the institute also provides a training in Big Data Hadoop and Data Analytics certification. The cost of their 'Digital Marketing' program is about 60000 INR.

The institute has an average student rating of *3.4/4* out of 15748 reviews on Google.

Digital Vidya is also an official training partner for Google.

- ***Enrol in a free Digital Marketing Course***: In case you are not willing to invest on a digital marketing course due to some reasons, you can always go for a "Free digital marketing course". There are a few websites which offer a digital marketing training, free of cost. Although the course is not in-depth, yet it is worth investing your time on. A few websites which offer this free course are, as mentioned below:

- *Digitaldeepak.com*: Few years ago, I started learning digital marketing from digitaldeepak.com. Initially, I started reading his blog posts, eventually I enrolled in the 'free digital marketing course' which contains 25 video lessons delivered on your email address every alternate day. After completing those 25 video lessons, you would also receive a certificate of completion.

- *Google Digital Unlocked:* There are 26 modules which comprises 103 video lessons in total. Each module has an assessment which you need to take in order to clear that module. All you need is to have a Gmail account to access these free video lessons.

- *E Marketing Institute:* You can also visit emarketinginstitute.org to enroll for a free digital marketing course, along with a 155 pages e-book and a certificate of completion. This course is suitable for beginners, as are the other similar courses.

- *soravjain.com:* Sorav Jain is a digital marketer, having organized more than 150 workshops across India on subjects like email Marketing, content marketing, Google Adwords, and so on. He offers you 30 hours of free digital marketing content on various topics like website building, SEO, content marketing. You can have free articles, e-books, videos, and digital marketing updates, once you enroll to his course.

- ***Go for an internship for a few months***: As you may already understand that you don't become a digital marketer, only by reading the blogs or any online content on digital marketing. You absolutely, need to practice it real time because companies look to hire those candidates who have some experience in one or the other aspects of digital marketing.

I understand that companies would not hire you full time, if you do not have a hands-on experience, however, you can always go for an internship for a period of 3 months/6 months to have a practical exposure to digital marketing. The best way to do that is to visit internshala.com and apply for various internships in your city.

- **_Practise it yourself_**: This method of practicing digital marketing, is by far, the best among the above few. All you need to do is have a 'self-hosted WordPress blog' and start implementing the concepts yourself to have a hands-on experience. There are various free online resources where you can learn concepts and the methods to build your own blog.

You would be able to gain practical experience in the form of a project that you can mention in your resume. The project can be your asset, that you can use to either monetize or make it a springboard to display your capabilities of handling digital marketing campaigns.

A blog is usually defined as an informative website on World Wide Web (www) consisting valuable information to your target audience on a specific niche. A niche refers to an industry segment e.g. Technology, economy, sports, travel, etc.

When I started blogging, I used to wonder what to write about and how to choose a topic for my blog. I started exploring the ideas to write one and came up with a couple of blogs, one on Automobile Technology and the other on Additive Manufacturing. Initially it was a challenge for me to set up a self-hosted WordPress blog. I would require having my own domain name and a web hosting plan to provide my blog, a home of its own rather than relying on free blogging websites like blog.com, blogger.com, medium.com, and so on.

Started a self-hosted WordPress blog has become easy now than it was few years ago. While I am writing this blog post, I understand what it takes to make my audience feel comfortable about starting a blog as I also used to be one of them a few years back. Now that I have gained a lot of experience in writing blog posts, I can share some ideas with you as well.

I would like to provide you some blog post ideas which can help you come up with a decision on choosing a topic easily. Here are some of the steps you can follow to get started on your blogging journey.

Choose a topic you are interested in

Choosing a topic has never been easy when it comes to writing and publishing that content on a website. A lot of people who aspire to be a blogger often quit because they are afraid to write and end up not even giving a try. The primary reason is the fear of a rejection by their audience and secondary being the lack of knowledge and self-confidence.

Think about what you are interested to talk about. Choose a "niche". Example: sports, politics, healthcare, technology, automobiles, and so on.

Alternatively, you can choose a "sub-niche". It could be; bicycles, luxury cars, mobile phones, culture, places, famous personalities, cricket, health, table tennis, or anything else you are passionate about.

Ask yourself what do you usually discuss with your friends or family? I am sure you would be able to come up with a topic and be one step closer to your blogging journey.

Try to analyze what your readers might want to read

A blog can be a piece of information which adds value to the people. It would be great if you could figure out what your audience might want to read. One of the ways to discover is by asking your friends and your colleagues what they like to read about.

Another way is by visiting forums like quora.com, reddit.com, etc. where you will find what are the things people usually interested to know. After the survey has been done, you would be able to find a "topic" which is an intersection of your interest and your audience's interest. You should aspire to be a leader of that niche by understanding your audience better.

Write eye-catching headlines for your blog

Unless you have a out-of-the-box headline for your blog post, nobody would bother to open your post and read it, even though your content is extraordinary and engaging for your target audience. A headline should be simple yet powerful. You can include these keywords in your headlines;

- "How to"
- "Why"
- "Top 10"
- "What is" , and so on.

Do some research before writing your first blog post

Look before you leap! Carry out some research on a topic you finally decide to blog on. There are various ways to do so. One of them is by visiting other blog websites and identify what they are writing and most importantly understand the structure of their blog post.

Read various articles on the niche you are interested and passionate about. Basically, you should understand three main things before you start writing a blog post; *Passion*, *Knowledge*, and *Demand*.

Write on a topic that can help solve your audiences' problems

Your audience would continue reading your blog only if they are gaining any valuable information out of it or if your entire blog or some of it helps them solve their problems. For example, if you are writing about automobiles, you can list out various troubleshooting methods that your audience can implement on their vehicle and help solve their problem. The most important objective to write a blog should be to help your "Target Audience".

Had I not shared valuable information for you here, you would not have been reading this right now! Hope I have clarified this point.

Include pictures as well as videos in your blog post

A content is "complete" when it contains text, images and videos. An image is worth 100 words written while a video is as good as 1000 words. Include relevant pictures and videos in your blog post, whenever possible. For example, you can use a video tutorial on "how to do something" or "how to make something more efficient".

Remember those school days when we used to feel bored of reading the content in the form of text, however we were excited to read the same stuff when the author would include some images as well, into it.

Research on your competition and implement

After you are done choosing a topic for your blog, go to Google and research on a few keywords that come to your mind and watch what websites appear on the search result. You would be able to make a list of your competitors in your niche.

The list will come handy in helping you understand how you can write an engaging content. But make sure you do not copy and paste someone else's content on your blog post, else you could be penalized by Google for doing so, and your self-hosted blog may also stand a chance to get suspended. Always use your own content; although you may refer your competitors' articles.

The act of stealing someone else's work is known as "plagiarism". After you finish writing your content, make sure you check it for plagiarism.

Ideally your blog should reflect 100% unique on plagiarism checker. You can also check grammatical errors on some of the plagiarism checker tools.

Check plagiarism on the following links;

https://smallseotools.com/plagiarism-checker

https://www.bibme.org/grammar-and-plagiarism

https://www.easybib.com/grammar-and-plagiarism

It took me a lot of time and patience to come up with a topic on which I could write a blog. It only takes "determination" to lead a goal to success. Hope this blog post would get you started on publishing your own blog post.

About a billion of people are consuming information (in one form or the other) over the internet. As the global economy is turning digital, it is essential for organizations to migrate to digital marketing. As more and more organizations are turning digital, opportunities in the field of digital marketing are increasing proportionally.

If you want to kick start your career in this booming industry, this is the time. The best way to learn digital marketing is not by learning the concepts but by practically implementing those, by you. In order to get a broad overview of what it takes to be a self-made digital marketer, you can follow the below steps to become a successful blogger.

- ***Choose a topic of your interest***: To start a blog on your own, you need to have a start. Think about something you are passionate about and start writing about it. Don't forget to include some images in your blog posts.

  Search for what people are looking to read over the internet and make use of that information to choose a topic to blog on. 'Quora' is one of the best platforms for you to have that information.

- ***Buy a Domain Name and a Hosting Plan***: To truly achieve blogging success, you must build a blog on your own domain name. A good domain name should ideally contain 8-12 characters and should ultimately help increase in the "Click Through Rate". Buy a shared hosting plan as per your budget and requirement. There are various cheap hosting plans available on the internet these days.

- ***Install a Content Management System***: WordPress is known as the best when it comes to a content management system. Usually employing PHP scripting language and MySQL Database, WordPress powers over 31% of the World Wide Web. Several hosting companies provide one click WordPress install. You do not require a coding language to build your blog, as there are various themes and plugins you can use as per your requirements.

- ***Start writing SEO Content***: A content should be created keeping S.E.O. in mind. Include the target keywords which stand a chance to coincide with the search query from your target audience. Don't worry if you are not good at writing; there is always an alternative. You can choose to outsource your content writing using "Content Mart". Click on *contentmart.com* and go register yourself. There will be plenty of people around, who can write content for you, at a minimal cost per word.

- ***Register and verify your property on Google Search Console***: For the search engine to identify your website and the corresponding pages in it, you have to let that engine know that your website exists.Google Search Console (formerly known as Google Webmaster Tools) is a free and a powerful analytics tool which provides an insight on what's happening on your website, the same way Google Analytics does.

  There are various ways by means of which you can verify your property (domain name) on a Search Engine like Google; The most common method is to copy the 'meta tag' and paste it onto your website's home page. The tag should go in the *head section,* before the first *body section*. To do this, go to your WordPress Dashboard, click on 'Appearances', followed by 'Editor'.

- ***Build your visitors' email list***: Once you build your WordPress blog, you will start receiving traffic, via both direct traffic and organic search. Unless you have a 'Call-To-Action" integrated on your website, there is no point of getting high traffic or any traffic for that matter.

  The ultimate goal of a 'Digital Marketer' is to monetize the blog with the introduction of its own products or services. To monetize the blog, we would require the information of our website visitors in the form of email address and/or phone number.

  There are various tools available to help you capture your visitor's contact information and build your email list, e.g. Pop-ups, header bars, etc.

  - ***Try Paid Marketing campaigns to promote your Blog***: Open an AdWords account and try paid campaigns; get started with low *Cost Per Click* bids. Google AdWords also provide free credit for new sign-ups. Also make some keyword research to observe what people are looking for, over the internet.

There are various *keyword research* tools, available online. Some of which are mentioned below;

Google Keyword Planner by which you can also get search volume for a list of the keywords and also the traffic forecasts from that keyword list. You can also discover new keywords and compare keyword trends.

https://ads.google.com/intl/en_in/home/tools/keyword-planner/

Moz Keyword Explorer offers free 1 month trial to identify the volume of the keywords along with the insight on difficulty, opportunity and the potential score.

Google Correlate helps fetch related phrases in conjunction with your primary keyword.

- ***Promote your content on social media***: Social Media is one of the strongest strategies to market, when it comes to promoting online business; Blogging is none other than a business. If you want to achieve success in blogging, treat it as a business.

Social Media campaigns have specific goals which are measured using Analytics, that help re-design those strategies like any other medium of marketing like GoogleAds, e-mail marketing, and so on.

In order to learn Social Media Maketing, the best way is to do it by yourself. Refer various articles on how to open a facebook page, other than your personal one, and how to promote your blog using Facebook advertising. Also embed social sharing buttons on your blog using wordpress plugins(for free). Similarly, you can also start promoting your blog using other social media networks like *Twitter*, *Pinterest*, Instagram, *LinkedIn*, etc.

- ***Register for a Google AdSense and an Affiliate Program***: Google AdSense allows the publishers (Website Owners) to serve automatic text, images, videos or any other interactive media. It is a *Cost per Click* advertising platform where any publisher who wants to put Ads on its website can register with Google AdSense program.

Joining Google AdSense is free of cost; Infact, Google would pay the publisher for every click or the impressions for the Ads you display on the website. Lets understand how it works;

An advertiser creates an Ad and asks Google to publish that Ad, either on the search engine or in Google's display network. Once you register for an AdSense program, you would be a part of that display network.

- *Create an AdSense account and activate it.*

- *Set-up AutoAds on your website.*

- *Set-up your account information for payments.*

- ***Sell your own digital product or service***:

Creating your own product or a service and promoting the same online, is by far the best you could do as a blogger. You can offer a lot of services or products to your visitors and make a good revenue that way.

A product can be an e-book, a course, etc. while a service can be website design, content writing, S.E.O, and so on.

Selling your own product or a service not only creates a revenue for you but also motivates you to write more and promote more, which is very important from a blogging perspective.

To build a self-hosted WordPress blog, the first thing you should have is a 'Domain Name'. A domain name is your web address which allows people to navigate and access your web pages. Just like your residential address, a domain name is also an address. Hosting, on the other hand, makes your website, visible on the "world wide web (www).

In case you are planning to have your WordPress blog, and want to make it accessible to your *target audience*, having a domain name and a web hosting is necessary.

Before starting my first blog (website) in the year 2012, I explored various domain name providers and hosting companies to make my blog accessible to the target audience. Since I was only trying to experiment with my WordPress blog to learn digital marketing, I did a lot of research on cheap domain and hosting plans. After having set up a few blogs over a span of 6 years, I finally came across a few companies who provide cheap domain name and hosting plan, a beginner should go for.

- ***GoDaddy***: The company provides various services including Domain Name, Hosting, Website Builder, Online Marketing including email marketing, S.E.O, and so on. You can host only 1 website on their 'Economy Hosting Plan'

  They offer a package (Hosting + Free Domain Name) which is yours till 1 year, and you get it for just <u>1400 INR</u> including all taxes.

  To avail this offer, you can follow these few steps;

  - Go to in.godaddy.com/Domain-Name/Hosting.
  - Choose your domain name.
  - Add a hosting plan (99 INR/month).
  - You will be directed to the Check-Out page.

- Complete your payment.

- You are done!

The customer service of GoDaddy is exceptionally good. I would strongly recommend you go for it.

- **_1&1 Internet_**: 1&1 is a web hosting company, based out of Germany. They have unbelievably good plans for Domain Name and Hosting. Just like GoDaddy, they also offer a free domain if you purchase any of their shared hosting plans. If you are a beginner,

  I would recommend you go for the _1&1 Basic_ plan which they offer for just 0.99$ per month, amounting to approximately 67 INR per month.

Unlike GoDaddy, '1&1 Basic' plan offers you;

- 100 GB storage

- 2.5 GB RAM

- 25 GB SSD (Database)

- Free Domain

- SSL Certificate

- 24/7 Service

- Page Load Time of 2.71 seconds.

I am using their hosting service, and am satisfied. Even though they have customer service phone numbers based out of United States, I was not able to establish a connection to those few numbers.

Apart from that, their services are exceptional!!!

- **_Hosting Raja_**: Among other cheaper 'Hosting & Domain' package providers, hosting raja also offers shared hosting plans starting from 98 INR per month, if you go long term (5 years). If you choose to separately buy a domain name and a hosting service, go for their starter plan, they offer for INR 65 per month, again if you go long term (5 years).

I would recommend you going for a Silver Pack which offers;

- 100 GB web space

- Host 3 websites

- Host 5 sub-domains

- 20 GB Bandwidth

- Customer Support

If you want a free '.in domain' along with the hosting, go for their gold plan, which offers 120 GB web space, and you can host 5 websites. Choose 1-year plan instead of going long term (more than a year).

They offer _Silver Plan_ for 129 INR per month, while their _Gold Plan_ is offered at 149 INR per month.

- **_Nextra Online Services Pvt Ltd:_** Headquartered in New Delhi, Nextra provides Domain & Hosting services, along with website building and email services. They are offering the following hosting and email services, at discounted price;

  - Free domain with C Panel Hosting + SSL + 5 emails at 89 INR/month
  - Windows Hosting (10 GB) starting at 762 INR/year
  - 50% FLAT OFF ON VPS Linux- starting at 798 INR/month
  - Dedicated Servers at 20% Flat Off.

You can go to their website, www.nextraone.com and try to connect with their chat team. They would ask your contact details followed by a call back with a discount code to avail the offer.

- ***go4hosting:*** Like other hosting companies, go4hosting also provides shared hosting, V.P.S hosting, and a dedicated server. If you have a budget upto 150 INR/month, you can go for their shared hosting plan, on a tier 3 data center. They offer three types of shared web hosting plans, namely; Home Plan, Basic Plan and Value Plan.

  All these plans include;

  - *Unlimited Disk Space*

  - *Unlimited web traffic*

  - *Unlimited e-mail support*

  Go4hosting has an average Google rating of *4.5/5 from 353 reviews*, which seems good.

Once you select the 'Home Plan' for a period of 1 year, you will need to either register for a new domain or if you choose to buy a domain name separately, go ahead and add that domain name on the box.

You can go ahead and choose one of the above mentioned hosting service and Domain name plans, and start your blogging journey!

S.E.O stands for search engine optimization, and is nothing but a way to improve the search ranking of your website or a blog for every search query by an internet user related to your business or a blog. S.E.O is a continual process and in order to maintain the same or higher ranking on the search engine result page (S.E.R.P), you must optimize your website or a blog regularly.

As Google search ranking algorithm keeps on updating, the S.E.O strategy that would have worked for you in the past may or may not work for you, now. You should also aim to build an S.E.O strategy which has a long term goal.

Before we leap into the steps to improve your organic website ranking, let's understand how search engine ranks a web page based on the search query from an internet user?

Let's assume that an internet user wants to read about "Top 10 IT companies in India". While there are 20 bloggers who have written a similar article on their website; In that case, search engines will rank these websites according to the two main parameters namely Relevancy and Quality.

While Relevancy Signals are offered by the Google Webmaster, the Quality Signals are provided by the users who visit your website. The relevancy signals are a part of an on-page S.E.O and the quality signals are a part of an off-page S.E.O.

How does Google find out that your webpage is the best against the internet users' search query?

Let's use the above example; when a user looks for information on the Top 10 IT companies in India, Google fetches thousands of search results based on that query.

Now let's assume that you have written an article on "Top 10 IT companies in the world". Google webmaster would not include your result on the first few pages of the search results, as your article is not relevant to the user's search query.

This process is called an 'On-page S.E.O' and these relevancy signals are provided by Google Webmaster tools, also referred as 'Search Console'.

Let's take another example where people are looking for "Top 10 digital marketing institutes in India" and there would be various bloggers who would have written a similar article matching that search query. Now in this case, Google would rank the search results based on the 'Quality Signals' it receives by the user behaviour. This way of optimizing the blog for SEO is called an 'Off-page SEO'

Below are a few ways which can help you improve your WordPress blog for SEO.

- **Content Management System**

I keep on mentioning that WordPress is the best content management system out there, when it comes to your website architecture. So if you are blogging on WordPress, you don't need to worry about the technical side of it. Wordpress comes with thousands of plugins which can help you optimizing your website for SEO.

So, go ahead and install wordpress for your website or blog, if you haven't already.

- **Web Hosting**

Fast page load speed substantially affects the SEO of your blog. By choosing the best hosting service providers who can ensure that the website uptime is at least 99%, SEO would not be affected. I have done a lot of research on various web hosting service providers and have written a separate article on that.

- **Quality Content**

The most important part when it comes to SEO is the quality of content on your blog. You need to make sure that you are writing good quality content as the search engine track user behaviour landing on your website e.g. time spent on the site, social shares, number of back links, etc.

Once you start offering valuable and relevant information to your website users, they would come back to your blog and would read more, however, in case a user clicks on your website URL on the search result page and exits without going through the information or if did not find the content on your website as useful as they desired, your website would start ranking lower as compared to other websites with a similar content.

The best way is to write a content, as unique as possible, and free of any grammatical error. It is also advisable to keep posting the articles once in a while to help the search engine keep crawling your blog resulting in improvement in the SEO.

- **Identify what your audience wants**

Once you build a blog on a WordPress platform, you can form a Facebook group wherein you start receiving questions from your website visitors. Based on those questions, you can write an article and solve their queries and at the same time, you stand a chance to build a trust among those visitors, thus helping boost the SEO.

You can also identify the search queries by the internet users from Google Search Console. Go to search console and click on your property (your website URL), and click on "Search Traffic" and the dropdown would appear. Now click on "Search Analytics". It would show you which keywords your website showed up for, but the users did not click.

As long as you keep on answering your visitor's questions and keep publishing articles which you think your website users might want to read, you can get the desired traffic to your blog.

- **Heading Tags(H1, H2, H3, etc.)**

Heading tags are the HTML tags in the form of a code which conveys your browser how to display your content. Heading tags also contribute in the ranking of your website on the search engine results. Each page or a post can have multiple headings like H1, H2, H3, H4, and so on.

H1 tag is the first header and is considered the most important. H1 tag is used for the blog title on the header. H2 heading, on the other hand, is usually found on the 'Post Title', 'Comments Title' and the 'Sidebar'. H3 and H4 headings are used to separate the various sections of your article, the way I have done in this blog post and other blog posts. To choose a specific heading while writing a blog post, go to 'Format', followed by 'Blocks' and choose a heading type e.g H1, H2, H3, H4, etc.

- **Image Alt Text(Alt Tags)**

Alt text (alternative text) or Alt attributes provide a better image description to search engine crawlers helping them to index an image properly. In case an image fails to load properly, Alt tags would be displayed and would help the crawlers have a better understanding of an on-page image. The Alt tag of an image should specify what's on it and provides users with a text equivalent to images.

Introduction to Google Analytics

Google Analytics is one of the most powerful tools available, with the help of which we can track the user behavior on a website. It allows you to gather data about various quantitative aspects of your website, like the number of visitors per day/week, the number of user sessions, time spent by the user on each page, the location of the user, and so many other features.

You can access Google analytics dashboard by signing up for a Google account like Gmail. Once you verify your property (website) with Google, Google analytics would fetch a tracking id in the form of 'UA-*********-*'.

Now you can install a Plugin from the list of various available Plugins with WordPress and add the tracking code on the Plugin so that Plugin would add that tracking code to all the pages of your website, and your website would be all set to be tracked for an ultimate analytics data of your website users.

There are a variety of available user data reports on Google Analytics dashboard. I will go step by step to help you understand some of the features of this powerful tool;

Real-Time:

Google Analytics Real-Time reports fetch real-time website user behavior reports which helps the website owner to analyze the data according to the requirement and optimize the content accordingly. The real time reports comprise of the following:

Overview- As the name suggests, a real-time report shows the number of active users on a website

Locations- Analytics will show the location of your website users in real time.

Traffic Sources- In this section of real-time report, analytics will show the source of the traffic i.e whether the user came directly to the website or through a search query or through a referral.

Content- It shows the pages which are being browsed by the website users in real-time.

Audience:

This report fetches the website users' information in terms of demographics, interests, behavior, technology used, and so on. Lets discuss these one by one;

Active Users- The users active on your website for a desired period i.e for a day, a week, a month, etc.

Demographics- whether the users are male or female, and what age group do they belong to!

Interests- which pages are your website users, the most and the least active on!

Geo- This analytics data would fetch the location of your website users along with the language they use to communicate, e.g. English(U.S), English(U.K), etc.

Behavior- How engaging are your website users and what is the percentage of 'New Visitors' versus the 'Returning Visitors'. This data also shows the count of sessions, total number of sessions, and the total number of pae views for a set range.

Technology- Which operating system are your website visitors use(e.g. Google Chrome, Internet Explorer, Safari, etc.), and who are their Internet Service Providers(ISPs)!

Device- Whether your website visitors are using a computer, a mobile or a tablet to access your website!

Acquisition:

Acquisition makes a website owner have an insight on the source of traffic to acquire visitors to their website. The reports show the following metrics;

Direct Traffic- Direct traffic defines the number of users who directly visited your website, for a set range of date.

Organic Search- Organic Search report fetches the data of your website visitors who landed on your website by means of a search query on a search engine.

Social- Social Search report fetches the data of your website visitors who landed on your website from a social channel e.g Facebook, Quora, Google+, Twitter, etc.

Referral- Referral traffic is a method of reporting visits to your website, outside of the search engine.

Behavior:

Behavior reports suggest the overall visitor's behavior on your website based on the following metrics;

- Page views
- Unique Page views
- Average time on a page
- Bounce Rate
- Exit Percent

Based on the business objective of a website, the metrics in Google Analytics can be changed. The data can be also be extracted hourly, daily, weekly and monthly.

Site Content- This metric shows which page had the maximum views and which had the minimum. The report also fetches the following parameters apart from the common parameters like bounce rate, page views, unique page views, average time on page, etc.

Entrances Count, which is defined as the number of times visitors entered your website.

Percent Exit, which is the ratio of the number of exits to the number of page views.

Conversions:

Defining 'Goals' is an important component of any digital analytics measurement plan, and it can be divided into the following matrices depending on the business objective;

Goals- Goals are a versatile way to measure how well your site or app fulfills targeted objectives. You can measure conversions, or completion rates, for each Goal you set up. Combine Goals with Funnels to analyze user actions leading up to a Goal. If you set a monetary value for a Goal, you can also see the value of conversions.

Examples of Goals include;

- "Thank you for registering" pages.
- "Flight Itinerary" confirmations.
- "Download Completed" page.
-

E-Commerce- With the help of Google Analytics ecommerce tracking, you can compare sales data with your website analytics data like bounce rate, traffic sources, etc. Ecommerce tracking is a snippet of code you can include on your site or app to collect transaction data like product sales, purchase amounts, and billing locations, and connect it to your Google Analytics account.

With ecommerce tracking, you can better understand the value of your digital business. Use the Ecommerce Reports to segment and analyze your data, and discover relationships between your marketing campaigns, user engagement, and transactions.

Customization:

With the help of Google Analytics tool, you can create customized reports depending on your business goal. A website owner may or may not find a value in a particular metric. Let's suppose a business is more into lead generation, the 'page value' metric would not benefit, and that the business is more interested in other metric. That's when 'Custom Reports' come handy.

To create a custom report, click on 'Customization' followed by a click on 'Custom Reports', and then click on ' New Custom Report'.

Now, put a title name, e.g 'Traffic'.

Under Report Tab, you can choose whether you want to have 'Explorer', 'Flat Table' or 'Map Overlay'. You can add matrices to the report tab, e.g. 'Advertising', 'Social', 'Acquisition', and 'Behavior'.

You can also add 'Custom Dimensions' similar to the above report matrices, as per your requirement.

When you are done customizing the report you want to analyze, click on 'Save' and you would be able to see the custom report dashboard with the matrices you chose.

www.ingramcontent.com/pod-product-compliance
Lightning Source LLC
Chambersburg PA
CBHW070934220526
45468CB00005B/1774